The Pain Left Behind

Surviving a Suicide Loss

A Collection of Poems

DAXSON PUBLISHING

Praise for: The Pain Left Behind

"There is no formula, timeline, or coping mechanism for grieving, and Erica Castro's poetry demonstrates the raw suffering and healing journey that one's spirit goes through during tragic moments. These words are an offering to break taboos, transform thorns into roses, and honor a beautiful life."

Rosalilia M. Mendoza
Author of: *Lily of the Valley*

Erica's poetry vulnerably dives into the complex, raw emotions following a loved one's suicide, revealing the indescribable pain and melancholic beauty in memories of those gone too soon. She offers a voice to those forced into the "Suicide Club," a group no one wishes to join, highlighting the spectrum of grief and loss that forever alters relationships and immerses survivors with guilt. Through her work, and the complicated nature of grief, Erica's poetry is a profound exploration of the continuous cycle of guilt and the relentless quest for healing in the aftermath of suicide.

Wynter L. Eddins
Author of: *After Glow*

Erica allows you to revisit bandaids as she holds your hand sharing an empathic connection of self, strength, loss, and healing. *Amends,* we as humans don't often allow ourselves to be human. We take the shape of our fears. However, Erica displays the embodiment of emotions through the cycle of grief due to suicide loss. She is granted the serenity to change what she can, understands the meaning of courage and loss, and is the wisest at knowing the will of temptation versus the strength to keep going.

VOTH | Voice of the Harbor
Author of: *Dieagnosis*

In her poetry, Erica offers her honest vulnerability and heartlfet reflection of her journey navigating through the grief of losing a loved one to suicide. From the darkest moments of grief eating away at our spirits alone, to all the times of not being able to crawl out of bed because the world has changed, and the days when no one truly sees us and understands the pain. Erica shows us that we are not alone. Her words invite empathy and compassion to everyone left behind after suicide and those who struggle with mental health. Her book is a friend that walks with the reader together in what happens next after picking up the pieces and finding the courage to move forward.

Jasmine Lan

In Erica B. Castro's collection *The Pieces Left Behind: Surviving a Suicide Loss*, every portrait of grief emerges raw, poignant, and relatable. After experiencing such tremendous loss, Castro bravely depicts how grief clings to us no matter the pressures of the to-do list or the longing to reconnect with friends and family. Poems like "I Didn't Drink," "Emotional Hangover," and "In the Clouds" entangle emotions of anger, guilt, and sadness with the glimmer of hope and truth that can come from such immense heartache. "Please Listen," "Double Loss," and "Don't Feel Guilty" invite better ways for readers to support others mourning a suicide loss. *The Pieces Left Behind* is a reminder that bereavement is unique to the individual. This collection emboldens readers to feel no shame for their grief and to no longer remain hidden in their pain. Castro's pen proves that poetry is a pathway through the storms of sorrow toward the miracle rainbows of healing that one day surprise us when we write it so.

Alex Petunia
Author of: *Tending My Wild*

We don't talk about grief. We don't talk about suicide. We definitely don't talk about suicide grief. This is what makes Erica Castro's collection vital, opening up the space for us to feel and heal through insurmountable pain. Her poems are raw, candid and vulnerable, as she takes us on a journey of grieving her loved one. If you have lost someone to suicide or know a loved one who has, this book is for you. It's a guide and a balm for the soul. In a spectacular tribute to her loved one Castro reminds us of the power of poetry and storytelling -- "And in these poems // You live on / Healing the world." I am grateful to witness how tenderly these poems carry grief and know each word is medicine our world needs.

Karo Ska
Author of: *Loving My Salt-drenched Bones*

The Pain Left Behind

Surviving a Suicide Loss

A Collection of Poems

Foreword by: Dr. Ken Schemmer II, DMin
By: Erica B. Castro

The Pain Left Behind
© 2024, Erica B. Castro
ISBN: 9798990053151
Library of Congress Control Number: 202491213

Cover Photo by: Leonard Carrillo
Graphic art by: Lola Rose Fernandez

First Edition, 2024

Printed in the United States of America

Edited by Kimiko White
Cover Design by Rachel Kiskaddon
Layout Design by Rachel Kiskaddon

Published by: Daxson Publishing Los Angeles, Ca, 90022

Dedication

I dedicate this book to all the people in the world who have walked my journey and who have lost someone to suicide. You are not alone.

Foreword

Poetry is one way that a person can connect to one's feelings on grief. Erica has written this poetry book that I believe has helped her discover her feelings about her loss due to suicide. I think also that this book could help you to find your feeling of loss due to suicide. I have led many grief groups, especially the one I currently lead due to the loss of suicide, through the *With Hope Foundation*. Any time you can read or write to connect to your feelings, you will discover your grief and start working through your grief journey. I find that the grief journey is not about forgetting your loved one, but working through the heartache. I love poetry because it can help you express your feelings, unlike other ways that don't quite connect to your heart.

Thank you, Erica, for your writing on this subject. You are brave to put into writing what your heart is feeling. I pray this will help others connect to their feelings on this painful subject. I also pray that it will help them start the healing of their heart from the loss of their loved one due to suicide.

Dr. Ken Schemmer II, DMin
With Hope, The Amber Craig Memorial Foundation
Director of Bereavement Services
kens@withhopefoundation.org
www.withhopefoundation.org

Table of Contents

Acknowledgments

I want to thank all the people who have believed in me and have supported me in my journey. I am forever grateful for the love and support of all the people who helped me out of the darkness and held me with their unconditional acceptance and love. My Infinite Poets, I would not be where I am without you. You have all etched a little piece of my heart, and I am so grateful for your love and support. Thank you for breathing belief in me when I did not believe in myself. My first CLI teachers Karo and Alex, I am forever grateful for the opportunity to have been mentored by you. My new teachers James Coates and Lisa Montagne thank you for all your insight and teachings. I am a better poet because of you. To my work sisters from the Schurr High School English Department, thank you for always being there for me, and putting up with my eccentricities. You all have been my cheerleaders from the day we met until now. I am forever grateful that destiny made us friends. Dr. Ken Schemmer II, DMin, thank you so much for serving the suicide survivor community by leading groups I appreciate you so much. To my beautiful and strong sister, Jessica, God knew what he was doing when he chose you to be my sister. You have pulled me through the mud and pushed me to keep going. Thank you for every time you pushed me not to quit. To my middle brother, Javier, I am so grateful for you because you have always been there for me, and I would not have wanted my journey in life to be without anyone but you. To my oldest brother,Tony, thank you brother because you took care of me when our father had to work, and I am forever grateful for all you sacrificed in being our caretaker. Thank you to Mikey and Lupita both of you make my life so much fuller because you exist. My precious Isabel no one has ever loved me like you.Thank you for all your love. Dante, Rhiannon, Leonard James, Melody, and Daniel thank you for your patience and support. I know there were times I could not be there for you because I was following a dream, but thank you for understanding and supporting me. Daisy, to my daughter in law, thank you for being such an amazing mother to my grandkids. I am so grateful God chose you to marry my son, and I would not pick anyone else to raise my beautiful grandchildren. Thank you for all you do. I really appreciate you. To my beautiful grandkids Azalea, Easton, and Daxson grandma loves you. Leonard, the man in my life, I would not be able to pursue my dreams if it were not for you and for that I am eternally grateful.

Preface

I want to warn everyone that this book is filled with heavy emotions, and it may cause people to be triggered. I do urge you to take your time, and step away if any of the content in this book is too much for you. This book is about my grief, and my struggle with suicide loss. My life forever changed after this type of death, and I will never be the same again. In life there are sometimes moments of before and after. For example, your life before you had kids, or before you were married, and your life after those events happening. For me personally, this loss has divided my life into a before and after. Before a suicide loss broke my soul, and after learning to live with the empty hole. Life for me has been a daily struggle because of this loss. For me it is not depression, I have lived in the pangs of depression and it is nothing like that. For me, grief hits in unexpected moments and the emotions may range from a few tears running down my face to wailing in screaming on the floor in a fetal position. I have bouts of anger with God, and I struggle to keep my faith after this loss. I was isolated and did not want to be around people, and I walked alone a lot of the time because I felt nobody could understand my pain. I would be surrounded by people and felt so alone, and at other times I could not speak my pain to others. Grief would hit me in unexpected places, and I had to learn to be gentle with myself and accept the journey I was now on. The guilt has sucked a lot of joy from my life, and the what ifs have tormented me over and over again. At times, I would beat myself up thinking what could I have done differently, but no amount of guilt I carry could reverse time. As difficult as it is, I have to reach acceptance, and as of now I am not there yet. I disagree with this death, and I am not at a place of acceptance. Although, I do go to suicide survivor groups for healing and support, as of right now I have not reached the point of acceptance. I hope you can take this journey of grief with me in hopes you can understand the people around you who have lost a loved one to suicide and be present with them in their grieving process.

xx

Introduction

I have written this book because I have lost a loved one to suicide. This experience has been the worst tragic event that has ever happened to me. I have suffered tremendously, and nothing compares with the pang of desperation that I am still living through with this loss. I wrote this book because what I have found is that many people do not understand how suicide loss is different than any other loss. Simply, because there is guilt attached to the loss. Our logical brains blame us for this tragic loss, and the only people who truly understand the pain are those who have directly suffered this type of loss. I have attended suicide survivor groups since the loss, and I have found that many of us struggle with the same things. A lot of people do not understand our grieving process, and so we are told "Get over it," "Move on," "he or she is in a better place," or worse they say, "I am not equipped to help you." As a result, we lose friendships, and relationships because people do not understand. I write this book that maybe this book can give insight into the suffering and grief a person experiences when they lose a person to suicide. We are not asking our friends and family members to heal us, we understand that is our job. However, we do look for unconditional support, and acceptance as we navigate the intricate process of surviving a suicide loss. I hope people read this book, so they understand how to be there for someone like me, and to those who have suffered a suicide loss know, "you are not alone."

The Pain Left Behind

Surviving a Suicide Loss
A Collection of Poems

Grieving in Silence

The hardest thing in the world
Is to grieve in silence
Wanting to scream yell wail
But I must hold it in

With just two tears
Running down my face
Knowing that it is not a place to grieve
I am in a work meeting

I wipe the tears
Put on my fake smile
And keep it together

A co-worker sends a text
Are you okay
I'm fine
I have been saying that
A lot lately

I am fine I am fine
I am fine I am fine
I will never be completely fine
I lost a loved one to suicide

I will forever live
With this empty hollow
Struggling to keep my
Head above water

Guilt knocking me
Down over
And over again

How dare anyone say,
You should move on
Don't feel guilty
She is in a better place
She would not want you to be sad

I do not want to hear that

I miss her

Her laugh
Her smile
Her sarcasm
Her essence
I miss how she loved me

Don't tell me love transcends
Time and space

I want her here

Grief from Suicide
previously published in: Graceful Growth by: Erin Baer and Kim White
Guilt is like ants that overtake my mind
Thoughts and thoughts of what I should've
Could've done
These ants torment my soul

The ants travel down to my heart
Pain in my chest
They multiply
Not like a heart attack
Not like anxiety
My heart has been beat up–bruised

The ants overtake my stomach
I feel nauseous like I want to throw up
I long to overeat
But I cannot eat
The ants are still there

The ants travel to my back
The muscle spasms
The unbearable pain
Not even ibuprofen can numb

Ants bred by suicide
Ants that overpower my body
Ants that cause me pain,
But do not answer why

I've lost a beautiful soul to suicide
And I can't emotionally accept
It does not make sense
Waves and waves of pain

Ants that contaminate my foot
I walk it hurts
I cry it hurts
White knuckling life
I need hope

I cannot live
With such pain
The ants have overwhelmed
My heart, body, and soul

The ants travel to my throat
I cannot eat
And I feel like they are eating away
At my insides
I have been voiceless for so long

No one understands
Are you over it yet…

I finally scream
I wail with a tidal wave of emotion
And tears
Why Why Why
These damn ants
They don't leave me alone

A gaping hollow in me
That can never be filled
Because I have to live
And this beautiful soul is not here

I Didn't Drink

You took your life
And I didn't drink
A miracle from heaven

Never in my life
Had I lived through
Such unbelievable pain

My insides were pulled out
My organs were hurting
My heart was barely beating

My lungs were jammed
I had to learn
How to breathe

The wind got knocked out of me
I fell to the floor
Like a child

Kicking and screaming
Tantruming
Blubbering

Why
Why
Why

And still in the midst
Of all my anguish
A symbol from God

I didn't drink

I wanted so much to drink
That is how an alcoholic
Like me

Responds to such hurt
But I would dishonor you
If I chose to drink

And showed that woman
To your already grieving mother
That alcoholic woman

She lives inside me
Belligerent woman
Who you or your mom
Or my brothers or my youngest son

Have never met
And so in all my desperation
From your loss

An angel came down
Touched me
And gave me the courage
Not to drink

Self-Care Not

It's 3:00 pm on a Saturday
I haven't showered
I can't shower

My hair is matted
I have it wrapped in a tangled bun
I am in the sweats I slept in last night

And I have so many things to do
Trying to run errands
And it is raining outside

This is what it looks like
When the claws of *Grief*
Have been sunk deep in you

You try to act as if you are okay
But clearly visually I am not
It's like a deep depression

But different
Because it comes from sadness
Of suicide

A fake smile
Painted on my face
As I am trying to not break

If I could disappear
Not have a job
Not have responsibilities

Then maybe I can give *Grief* its time
Give it its space
So I can declaw *Grief* from my back

Nobody understands
In my circle
I get asked
Why are you crying

I hear this over
And over again
And all I can say is

It is just *Grief*

Grief reminded me she died
Grief reminded me I missed her
Grief reminded me that she loved me

Everybody says you need self-care
Groom yourself
Take showers and change clothes

But when *Grief* comes
It is a miracle to get out of bed
And try to get things done

Grief has no mercy
Grief drags you to the floor
And claws you in your heart

Maybe tomorrow
I can shower and brush my hair
And change my clothes

I can't self-care today
Because *Grief* came
And took over

Thursdays

From the moment you chose to die
Thursdays will never be the same
For weeks I had to brace myself
When Thursdays came

The memories of that day
Infected my mind
The words that were said
The fear of where you were

The worry of your well-being
The lying to myself
That you needed time away
And that you would be fine

Little did I know that
You chose to die
That you were not fine
And I would never hold you again

Thursdays haunt my heart
It was on a Thursday that
My life abruptly divided
Before and After became a reality

Before was when you lived
And this world had a ray of light
And joy filled my heart
And Thursdays made sense

After my life fell into a pit
I lived in the darkness of Thursdays
There was no hope
No joy and I was full of confusion

Thursdays are not just

Any old day of the week
It is the day I lost you
The day a storm cloud
Decided to follow me

Thursday became a day
that if I smiled or laughed
It became a sin
I do not deserve happiness

Thursday was the day that guilt
Rained and poured over me
And lightning struck

Thursday said,
You will never be the same
And I have not been well
Since that Thursday

Everyone says they hate
Mondays
But I
Hate Thursdays

For the rest of my life
For the rest of my breaths
For the rest of my heartbeats
For the rest of my time

I will move with this
Pang of pain in my heart
Reminding me
That you chose to die

On a fucken Thursday!

Scrambled Brain

Trying to get the kids to school
Packing lunches
Trying to get my things together

I feel this heavy desperation
In my chest
So I forget things

Things I so desperately need
To function at work
Like my glasses

I can no longer see up close
I teach and I need to read
Or my computer charger

How can I do my lessons
With a dead computer
Or without my notes

I have my teaching plans
I work so hard to put together
And I forget

Since you passed
I have a scrambled brain
Where I forget important things

I have forgotten appointments
I have forgotten commitments
I have forgotten meetings

All because grief gets in the way
Of me functioning
They say grief is connected to love

And through this process
And this scrambled brain
I realize I truly loved you

I cannot get you out of my heart
You live there with the love
You had for me

I cannot get you out of my mind
The memories we shared
When you lived

I cannot get you out of my body
We were kin
And we were connected by blood

My dearest girl
My brain is not the same
It is trapped in a grief frog

And it is scrambled
Because of the deep love
I have and will always have

For you

My Grief

I am human
my feelings
are meant to be felt
but most of the time
I want to numb out

sometimes when dealing with
uncontrollable grief
I want to run through it
as if nothing happened

nothing is really wrong

my heart was cut
into a mosaic of a million pieces.
and I have to still live

SUICIDE
a different type of grief
has brought me
to my knees

I have an emptiness
an unbearable
sense of desperateness
I can not cry

I am holding on to overpowering
emotions
refusing to let them go
emotions tied up in torrents

I can not
and will not
set myself free

for months

I have been struggling with life
holding everything in
no one could understand.
I am alone

not that nobody loves me
but no one close to me
knows what it is like to be me
so much suffering and nobody knows

I can not make sense
of the trauma submerging me
I have no will for self-care
dying for the pain to end

and yet still getting up
still trying to work
still trying to be a mom
still trying to care

and every moment
that passes
I am lost and wandering
trying to find my way
through this fucken complicated grief

You Do Not Understand

Please do not tell me to get over it
I have been in a grief prison
Like Alcatraz
Trying to detangle this barbed wire
That has me trying to function
Behind trapped doors

I am barely able to move
Every movement is painful
The barbed wire cuts me
As I am trying to escape

And yet you want me to do well in life

How can I do well
when I live in constant pain
I was not prepared to function
with such a deep hole

And yet I am still breathing
Still trying to move
Grief and sorrow consume me

How could this be my life
How long ago did she pass
Why does it still hurt
Were you even that close

Are you the depression police
Who thinks you have the right
To give grief a timeline
To give me a timeline

She existed
She breathed
She lived
She was supposed to have a life after 24

And I am supposed to be okay
I will never see her face again
I will never touch or hold her
I will never hear her laugh

The barbed wire is tightening
Yet I have to get up everyday
Living in this pain

Tears like a water spout that never closes
Oceans, and waves of grief
I am swimming
But I can't set myself free
Feeling like drowning

But I have to live

I have to honor her
Make her proud
Remember her
She now defines
My purpose
My existence

Depression of grief
Fabricates truth
Tries to say life in pain is no life

Today I am smarter
I will not be caught up in suicide's spell
I have to show that it can be done
That I can live with this grief
That my life is not over

That life is precious

Regardless of the darkness
Regardless of the hurt
That the only way
I can see the light

Is to feel the feelings
I will never be normal again
This is my new normal
Living with an empty hole

But I will feel love once again
I will find joy in nature

Appreciation
Passion

In the midst of all the pain

Damn it, do not tell me to get over it
I am here
I am living
I am doing the best I can

Losing You

My life is not the same
Since you chose to die
My heart has been crumpled
And it hurts to live

When you died
You took pieces of me with you
You took my positive outlook
I struggle to see the bright side
Today

You took my happiness in a way
I was told happiness is a choice
And it has been damn hard
To choose happiness

I will never be the same
Because those pieces are gone

They say I should be grateful
But my logical mind
Stops me from having peace

It says you should have stopped her
It's your fault
You did not see her silent battle
It says you are responsible for this pain

Guilt swallows me whole
And there are days
That repeat in my mind
Of things that could have been

I just wish I could go back in time
And do things different
Draw a sign in the sky

To tell you how much you mattered
And how much I loved you

I wish I had a magic wand
Or the magical healing cream
And pull your hurts from you
And set them free

I wish I could have
Warmed your anger
Made you understand
Let you scream
Give you voice
Maybe you would have had peace

I wish I could have had the list
Of all the people you touched
All the people that loved you
And all the people whose life was better
Because you existed

So you could see sweet girl
You left behind droplets of light

Because you loved
You cared
And your heart uplifted others

This grief of missing you has been
My hardest mental health battle
Nothing compares to the sorrow
I carry because you are gone

The only glimmer of hope I have
Is the gratitude I have
For having had the privilege
Of knowing you

SUICIDE

Stripped of what used to be my habitual life
Unleashing monumental grief and anger
Impatiently waiting for this pain to subside
Crying uncontrollably asking why
Imagining your last moments over and over again
Dearest soul of my heart life is too long without you
Every single moment that passes I ache for you

Abcedarian Poem on Suicide Loss

And just like that a mountain of grief crushed my diaphragm
Breathing has been difficult it has become a
Chore--the altitude is too high and trying to take in oxygen is something
Deemed out of the question because
Every single day I think of you--sometimes every moment--you are
Forever carved in the nucleus of my cells
Gutting my insides out--I carry an empty
Hole--a hole that has often tried to bury my soul
Igniting a fire of anger and hurt
Jailing me in my grief
Keeping me stuck below this mountain
Living a hollow existence
Making getting out of bed and showering impossible
No--I cannot set myself free--I am guilty
Open-ended grief--there is no way out
Pretending I'm ok--but submerging in a
Quagmire of what-ifs
Reliving your death--over and over again
Seeing that movie in my head--of the last
Time I saw you--I was so proud you
Unlike any other time--you just came back from boot camp
Villainous depression that stole you from me
Wondering where is the grace
Xenon gas overpowering my pores--gasping--gasping--for air
Yelling crazily--this is totally unfair
Zillions of times--I have the thought is there something I could
have done

Double Loss

People come into your life
For a reason
Sometimes for a season
And few are there for life

We were friends since childhood
It was you who pushed me through
The loss of my mom at age five
You were always optimistic and hopeful

When I was divorcing
It was you who said something better is coming
You believed in me
When no one else did

Things seemed so simple for you
It was as if you psychically knew
I was going to be okay
And you were going to be there every step of the way

For years I could call you
And you could call me
And we were soul sisters
No matter what was happening

Unexpectedly I suffered a suicide loss
I looked for you
I called for you
And all of a sudden you were no longer there

You did not take my calls
And in social settings
You avoided me
You were no longer my best friend

Lost and confused
It was always you that helped me through
I had just lost a loved one
And now I lost you

Finally after months
I confronted you
And you said,
I am not equipped to be there for you

What were you saying to me
I could no longer be your friend
Because your grief was too much
I do not want to be your friend because she died

Were you saying
Your crazy
And I cannot handle your crazy
I need to protect myself
From your grief

I could not understand
How you abandoned me
When I needed you most
I did not need you to rescue me

I just needed you to see me through
To believe in me like you did before
To hold my hand
and say it will be okay

You will survive
You always survive
But I was alone
Because you were
Not equipped to be there for me

The suicide loss
Was not my fault
Yet I felt as if you punished me
For hurting and grieving

A year and six months
Have passed
And I see now
You were not really my friend

Friends don't abandon friends
When you need them most
They do not give you lines like
I am not equipped to help you

True friends love you
No matter what

The silver lining is
At least this suicide loss
Showed me who you really are
And I do not need friends like that

I Can't Go

I know you are tired of inviting me
Because I always say I can't go
I do not mean to tell you no
But my heart has been suffering lately

And I can't go
I can barely do the day-to-day
Necessities in life
And I am not really up for questions

I can barely handle
My responsibilities
And trying to be present
With those who still live with me

I do not mean to cancel on outings
Or holidays
Grief has overpowered me
And I barely can function

I cannot be around people
I feel guilty if I feel happy
Or laugh
How can I do that when she is gone

I do not want to sour your moments
You deserve to have fun
You deserve to be happy
I just can't go

I can't go
I can't go
I can't go
I can't go

Just daily living is too much
And if I am going to keep moving
I need you to love me
And understand

This is not personal
It is not about you
But just right now
Grief has a hold of me

I am working through
Slowly
I want to keep going
So I need your support

You my loved one
My friend
Who loves me so much
Please understand

I just can't go

Dark Cup

They say that we all have cup
And we chose for the cup to be full
Or empty
That happiness is a choice
And that life is what we make of it

Tell me then how do you fill a cup
When you are suffering never-ending grief
One year six months and your suicide
Stripped the hope I had for joy
And the empty dark cup became normal

Left with never-ending questions
What ifs infect my mind
The emptiness of not having you near
And yet I have to still carry this empty cup
Still trying to live life

Not knowing if I will ever see you again
Or feel the way you loved me
The way you brightened my life with your smile
My precious loved one
How do you make sense of what is impossible

I will never know

why your cup was dark and empty
why you pretended it was full
why you chose to suffer alone
why I was not there for you

Today I carry a dark empty cup
Not because I want to die
But because I am grieving your loss
Angry at God
Angry at myself

Nobody seems to understand
I am not the same person
Your death has cut me to my core
I do not understand this grief
It feels like a life sentence
To carry around this empty dark cup

Because I will forever be living
With a missing piece
That died with you
And my cup will never have light
Or be full again because I lost you

Life is Heavy

Losing you was a shock to my psyche
I try to smile
But the heaviness makes me frown
I feel guilty when I have glimmers of joy
Life has been heavy

As if I punish myself for laughing
Because how can I be happy
Or laugh when you chose to die
I wasn't there to stop you
Life has been heavy

Just thinking about how much you suffered
And wondering how you felt to die alone
Wishing for miracles when we could not find you
Asking all the angels and God for help

But it was too late
You were already gone
Leaving a crowd of us in mourning
I can't seem to be happy anymore
Life has been heavy

Grief overruns my days
I am working
Trying to teach English
And all I can think of is you
Life has been heavy

I am at the store
Trying to fill my cupboards
I am getting ready to pay
Your nostalgic song comes on
Life has been heavy

Tears upon tears upon tears

I am driving home
I look at a young girl walking
I have to double-take
Because for one second
I thought it was you
Life has been heavy

I cannot seem to stop
The grief that is in me
It has life and it speaks to me
I feel like my life is behind bars

Never to be set loose
And I have not accepted
That for the rest of my life
Life will forever be heavy

Suicide Survivor's Club

I am now apart of this club
A suicide survivors club
I lost a loved one to suicide
And although death has diseased my life

Nothing compares to the grief of this loss
I lost my mom at five years old
I lost my dad at 27 and although it hurt
Nothing was similar to this type of loss

I wanted to go with her
And not be alone
But what she left behind
To all that loved her
Was mountains and mountains of grief

I know I am loved
My loss would be the same
And so I scream *Noooo*
I will not do the same
And leave those that love me behind

I have a seven year old that needs his mom
I have a daughter that cannot live alone
I have students that need my heart
I have poetic friends that need my poems

This club I now belong to
Has led me to people
Who know what it is like
To suffer this type of loss

Who know what it's like to lose friends
Or to be told inappropriate comments

Did you not see the signs?
She is no longer suffering
Or she is in a better place
Or you should be grateful
Get over it
She died along time ago
I am not equipped to help you
Don't feel guilty

This group knows this pain
Caused by people who have not had a suicide loss
This group has carried the burden of guilt
Just like me

Nobody knows what it's like
Unless someone you love chooses to die
And leaves you behind
Her pain was too much and she said goodbye

And now we
this suicide survivors club
Navigate this never-ending grief

In our groups

We don't tell you how to feel
We are entitled to speak and feel
We do not give you answers
We say what has worked for us

You are free to do grief your own way

And the only glimmer of light
Through this dark hole
Is we are not alone
And we are sorry for your loss

But above all we send you love
We are here with you

First Thanksgiving

How am I supposed to celebrate
And be thankful
It has been three months
Since you chose to die

I know we did not have
This holiday together
But I always knew
You existed somewhere

There was always
The Happy Thanksgiving intentions
And the I love you
And the I miss you

How I regret
Not spending enough time
Not texting you enough
Or hearing your voice enough

I regret not telling you
How proud of you I was
And that your voice always brightened up my heart
Or how grateful I was for you

I hate that I can't reverse time
So I could knowingly cherish
Every single moment with you
From the moment of your birth till your last moments

Forgive me my dear
I wish I could have done more
I loved you so deeply
I just wish I had more time

I had not cried like I did
On this first Thanksgiving
Deeply missing you
I left to the store

I went to the park instead
I wailed a primal cry
Wailed and wailed
And screamed

Your death
Hit me like a ton of bricks
I had not cried like this before
But it was the first Thanksgiving

A Thanksgiving
Without you in this world
And I realized this was truly the end
I would never see you in this life again

Shattered hearts
Lost time
Broken dreams
Disoriented thoughts

Thanksgivings will never ever be the same

Please Listen

Friends, family, confidantes
Have you ever heard talking it out helps
It takes the energy out of your body
And at least your spitting it out

And yet people do not understand
Grief makes you repeat
It makes you say the same story over and over again
It makes you speak it, speak it, and speak it again

Please do not tell me
You told me that already
I have never lived through this before
My loved one chose to die

And there is so much guilt
So much internal blame
So much personal responsibility
And the only thing I can do is speak on repeat

Why because that is the only way
I can try to make sense
Or try to understand
Or simply releasing grief from my body

I do not get it
I do not have answers
It is too hard to be alone
I do not accept it

I plead to you
Please listen and love
Hold my hand
And hug

And know this story
For months
For years
For my lifetime

Will be constantly told on repeat

So please be patient
Be kind
Be loving
Be understanding

I did not choose this
And I thank you
For being there
And still listening

Don't Feel Guilty

I was sad
And he asked what is wrong
I said I feel guilty she died

He immediately responded
Don't feel guilty
I swallowed my anger

I wanted to scream

If you have the formula
Give it to me
So it won't hurt anymore

If you know how
I can pull this from my being
Tell me

Because you act as if
I have not tried
As if I am perpetually suffering on purpose

I don't know how to not feel guilty
I don't know how to wrap her death
Around my brain

Don't you think I want to be free
Don't you think I want to stop blaming myself
If it was so easy to not feel guilty
I would

But I can't
I miss the life she should have had
The kids she would have raised

Please do not tell me

Don't feel guilty
I wish I could but I do not know how to

I looked into his eyes
And said
I'll try

So many people think
Guilt can be just turned off
It is an ever present battle

So many people think
We can just get over
A suicide loss

So many people think
We can just move on
But we can't

Please don't tell us
Not to feel guilty
We really do not know how to stop

Suicide Contagion

On September 27, 2013
I took sleeping pills while drunk
To try and end it all
I was alone

I felt like I had lost it all
I was a terrible alcoholic mother
My husband had left me
For another woman

I saw no reason to keep going
My pain was unbearable
And so I tried to die
And lived

I am grateful for the miracle of life
God saved me
And he could have let me go
I lived

It led me to find help
Out of the darkness
And to determine my own worth
From the goodness in my heart

Then you my sweet girl
Chose to die
And somehow deep inside
Of me

I wonder did I teach you that
Did you follow my bad example
Did you think it was easier
Because I once tried to die

Suicide my dear love
Was not the answer
My pain eventually ended
And I lived

This reality
Makes me angry at God
Because if he could save me
Why didn't he save you

They say suicide can be contagious
Did I contaminate you
My beautiful girl
Did I teach you wrong

I am sorry my dear
I was wrong
I live with emptiness today
Because you are gone

And in a second
We can lose it all
Life is too precious
To chose it to end

And suicide is not the answer
Because pain eventually ends
And what seems impossible
In that moment

Five years later is irrelevant

So stay strong all
You matter
You are needed
You are loved

PTSD

I did not see you
I was not there
When they found you
But when I was told

The PTSD started
I imagined myself with you
In that moment
Blood oozing

Me holding you
Screaming
Wailing
For help

But no one came
I could not stop the blood flow
I could not stop the physical trauma
I could not save you

I held you
And held you
And held you
And held you

They had to pry me off of you
I did not want to let go
Of your lifeless body
I was trying to hold on to your corpse

To see if by a miracle
I could take a little piece of you with me
But it was too late
You were gone

I was left with PTSD
I did not see it
But my brain imagined it
And I was there

Like a dream
Everything feels real
My senses sharpened
Heightened

I heard the sound
I saw the trauma on your body
I heard my screams
Calling for help

It did not happen
But in my brain
It did
And I was a witness

I saw life slipping out of you
I was too late
I wailed and wailed
I lost my sweet little butterfly

And I was left with PTSD

Suicide Sonnet

She was alone and no one heard her cries
Trauma from the recent past consumed her
She worked hard for peace she really tries
With a squashed voice there was no hope for her
She chose to die and left us here to mourn
Nobody knew the trauma existed
So she left us here desperately torn
Suffering torture the hurt persisted
Nobody understood we all were lost
How could someone so precious choose to die
Those deep secrets kept and what was the cost
One impulsive act and we still ask why
We lost a princess a precious loved one
Life was way too much and suicide won

August 11, 2023

I guess I am suppose to be happy
You got your wings a year ago
You have been giving me signs
Rainbows, hummingbirds, coins, lady bugs

I have to believe you are okay
As much as it kills me that you are not here
That you are gone
I believe you are up in heaven

Flapping your angel wings
Finally having peace
Nobody can hurt you anymore
You don't have to prove yourself

Your journey is done
And now your meeting
Your angel duties
Healing the world

Your angelversary is here
And it is hard for me to be happy
It is just that I miss you so much
And I struggle to see the light in this

So I trick my mind
And try to believe that you are happy
That you are with my loved ones
That passed before you

You are a real angel now
And every year that passes
I will always remember you
And try to be grateful that you are in the sky

As I try to navigate this hard road of grief
Trying to accept my new reality
The only hope is knowing
I have this precious angel watching over me

A precious blessing of my life

A Year Later

A year ago exactly
 they found your body
You had chose to die

No sign
No warning
No answers

A beautiful soul hurting
We were blinded by your smile
We thought you were happy
Because of your laughter
You always joked around

How did we miss it
Where did we go wrong
Why could we not see
That your beautiful dark eyes
Had a hidden sadness behind them

Since that day
I will never be the same
It is like I am trying to breathe
With damaged lungs
I am struggling to walk
With a hurt foot

How do you make sense
Of the impulsive
Of the irrational
Of the silent battle you were fighting
And nobody knew

How to go back to normal
When normal will never exist
Guilt filling my veins
No escape no freedom

Don't tell me not to feel guilty
You were only 24
Don't tell me to get over it
There does not exist a way how

The only thing you left me
Was the will to live
I witnessed the sorrow
I carry the pain
We all miss you dearly
But you gave me the will to continue to live

Lost Plans

Since I have lost you
My brain has become my enemy
Thought after thought
Vision after vision

Of what life was supposed to be
For you
I get polluted by images
Of what should have been your wedding

I think of the proud moments
You would have had in the National guard
Or your success at your job
The plans that never came

These plans were not lost
They were abruptly killed
And a dream that was supposed to be true
Ended

It is hard for me to live in the present
Because I get disoriented
By the belief of
What could have been

My brain sends me to the day
You would have been a mother
And held your child near
I could almost see your sweet gentleness

There are no answers to these thoughts
I day dream and imagine
The life that never was
And the joy you could have lived

And one more time
I fall down into the abyss
Trying to walk the convoluted road
Of wishing you were still here

I Can't Write

I am running out of time
My deadline to hit 100 pages
Is Monday today is Saturday
I have exactly two days to finish this book
And I have avoided writing like the plague

Who is crazy enough to write a book on suicide grief
When there is so much healing still needed to be done
Yet you sent me a rainbow today
To remind me of the importance of this book

My dearest one
I have been crying so much
This book has taken me to depths of pain
I never knew I was capable of

So much hurt so much pain
So many memories
So much loss
And yet you send me rainbows

To remind me
Keep going
It hurts and I cry
I want to wrap my arms around
You

I called your mom
And she laughed because it is so you
You would show up as a rainbow
And right before I could take a picture

You left and disappeared
As if to say get that book done

Thank you for coming
And showing me you're with me

That I am not alone
And you are walking
In this space with me
You have seen me cry

And still you love me
And urge me
Not to quit
People need to understand

I cannot write
But I need to write
I am running out of time
But this book is too important

To leave undone
Maybe it can give healing
Maybe it can answer questions
Maybe it can give peace

Either way my sweet girl
Stay with me
Because I cannot do this alone
Your loss has taught me so much

It needs to be spoken
It needs to be screamed
It needs to be taught
It needs to be shown

Thank you
For not giving up on me
Walking with me
And comforting me through the tears

This book will get done

Suicide Grief Performance

I performed the poems
The poems describing
The tearing of my heart
And the depth of your loss

The poems that make me cry
Because I miss you so much
And I wish I could go back in time
And show you more love

Even if I lost you when I did
I wish I could or would have
Appreciated the moments
I had with you more

I carry my biggest regret
Of not saying how much I really loved you
Not saying how proud of you I am
How important you were to me

Not that I could change anything
But just so that you could really know
How much you mattered to my soul
And how deeply you touched me

Even though
these poems scream my love for you
I wish I could have told you in life
Not now

So I scream my pain
About your death
To others so they know
To love their loved ones

And not take the beauty
In their lives for granted
Although my tears flowed,
While performing
I do it

To honor you
To remember you
To love you
To advocate for others

Hidden pain
Is real
Mental health demons
Exist

And if we share
Our suicide grief

Then we can tell others
They are loved and necessary
For this world

Poeting

I poet my grief
And scream
Maybe someone out there
Can hear me

I am not okay
I try to move through it
I can't it's too much
So I spill my hurt on the page

Maybe I am not alone
Through my words
Someone out there can see
Or listen and understand

This is what it's like to be me
I have moments of reprieve
Other times I'm on the floor
Crying wailing trying to catch my breath

I can't seem to control my grief
It comes in different moments
Different times
Almost always unexpectedly

And one more time
I become paralyzed
With grief
Wanting the world to stop

Yet I have to move
And move
And move
And move

I am seeing the world
Through a kaleidoscope
Distorted unclear
Confusing

Everyone around me
Is normal
Still living life
As if nothing has changed

I cant see clearly
Because this grief
Shows everything clouded
As if my eyes have cataracts

Grief devours me
So I poet my grief
And tell others
Your story

So that they know
To love
To care
To have compassion

Because we all need hope
So because of you
And the loss I suffered
I poet my grief

And tell the world
Love yourself enough
To speak your grief
And tell your truth

Unhealed mental health steals lives

Emotional Hangover

Have you ever cried so much
That you wake up the next day
Hungover

You didn't drink

But your body aches
Your head hurts
Your face is puffy

Grief can cause hangovers
Where you feel like
You have been hit by a truck

Grief has the power
To make you feel
Small

To make you feel
Submerged
With desolation

It steals hope
Burns joy
Covers you with guilt

Suicide grief
Is worse
Because logic torments your mind

Makes you believe

I could have done something
I could have said something
I could have changed something

It is different than any other type of death
Because somehow you feel like
You had some power to change things

But the truth is
The bottom line is
There was nothing that could be done

So you suffer these hangovers
Intertwined with despair
Mixed with questions

Trying to keep going
Through this undying punishment
of grief

Stop Telling Me I Am Strong

There are moments I want to quit
I no longer want to continue or breath
But I can't bare the thought of
My loved ones hurting because I am gone

So with an empty soul
I get my physical body up
Drag myself into the shower
Wash my hair and scrub my face and body

I am living an empty existence
But I keep going
I have a job
I have responsibilities

I have children
To get to school
To feed
To do their homework

I am hurting
But I try to keep moving
People look at me
And say you are so brave

Brave

How am I brave
Because I showered today
Because I made it to work
When all I want to do is hide under the covers

People say you are so strong
If you only knew how difficult it is
To get out of bed
To brush my hair and teeth

Yet I am brave and strong
You do not know
I cannot share
Because you are not safe

You do not understand
Suicide grief
You do not get
the constant piercing thorn of pain

It is a thorn that is growing
In my heart and I cannot speak
Or say a word
Because you do not understand

You have never lost anyone to suicide
And you say things like I do not know how you do it
How are you working
I would not be able to work

How can you say that
it has not happened to you
Thank God that you are not me
And you do not live pushing yourself
To breathe every step of the way

Do not tell me I am strong or brave
I live with incessant hurt
Do not be proud of me
I am suffering yet trying to keep breathing

I do not need to hear that from you
I am not brave or strong
I am just living empty
And still trying to breathe

I Still Believe in God

I am an alcoholic
Who is sober
It has been ten years
No alcoholic drink

God did not save you
Like he did me
And I have been angry

Although to stay sober
I need God
I have accepted

To agree to disagree
You should be here
With us thriving

Yet God said no
And although I cannot accept
Or I cannot have peace

I say to God
I disagree with your death
I know he knows better than me

At this moment in time
That is where I am
I cannot accept or agree

I am still angry at God
But I know he exists
Because he saved me

So this relationship
with God
Is bittersweet

Angry
because you died
Grateful because I lived

I know that acceptance
Is the answer
And God does not make mistakes

But I cannot at this point
Be in that head space
Of accepting the unacceptable

My loved one
A 24 year old soul
Chose to die

And in my logic
In my brain
I cannot accept

So for today
This moment
This second

I accept this
Disagreement
with God

I know He exists
But you should be here
With me

So I carry on
With this difference of opinion
Knowing I have to accept God

But dissenting with Him because of your death

Visiting hours

If I had a pass to see
One person in heaven
It would be you
I would just sit in your presence

I would feel
how you loved me
And you would feel
how I loved you

I would not waste time
on questions
I would just be grateful
I had one more moment with you

I would stare into your eyes
And feel so blessed
That I had the honor of
Spending time with you

I would say how proud of you I am
And I would say all the things I
Never got to say when you were here

I would remind you
how beautiful you are
I would try not to be sad

And not let you know
how much I have missed you
I would relish in the moment
And the blessing of having you near

If heaven had visiting hours
There would be no question
I would go to you

Give you my heart

And say thank you
For filling me with
Your laughter
For loving me so deeply

I am different because
You existed
Because you touched my soul
And showed me that I mattered

I want you to know
I remember your life
From the moment you were born
Till the day you died

I remember the beauty
You brought to me
And this world
The light you shined
And your smile that healed

I feel you in my heart
Even though you are not here
I have to believe one day
I will be with you again

Screaming your name
at the top of my lungs
And saying it is you
it really is you

In the Clouds

You're not gone
My tears show that I feel a loss
A loss that I can't seem to move through
A loss that has forced me to do life
In pain

My sadness seems annoying
To some
I am no longer always positive
And grateful almost bitter

In the deepness of my grief
I looked up at the sky
Trying to find your face
In the clouds

Realizing that you live
In their shapes
You live in the warmth of the sun
You breathe through the wind
When the trees sway

In the precious red rose
You stand on display
It's your beauty
You live

You sing through the birds
Those precious sweet sounds
Chirping at dawn
Reminding me of your voice

You fly through the butterflies
Going from flower to flower
Existing as their wings flap
With so much peace

Your colors shine
Through the rainbows
Saying hello
As you color the sky

My dearest one
I hate that you are not here
I hate that you are physically gone
But I have to remember you live

All is not Lost

It is hard to be grateful
We lost so many future years
When you chose to die
So many memories not done
So much hope that could have been

I am not saying your life here
Was not enough
Because in your short time
You changed the world

You changed my world
You gave me hope
When I had none
And it came simply from your love

You loved me unconditionally
You knew what it was like to feel like me
And I always knew you loved me
And that was enough to fill my life

Please understand your death
Will always be a tragedy
Because you left so many of us
Who loved you wounded

But I want you to know
You healed hearts
With your love
And zest for life

You were driven
Ambitious
Goal-oriented
And you had conviction

So you left your essence
In this world
And all is not lost
Although you are gone

You are honored
Remembered
Appreciated
And in these poems

You live on
Healing the world
By the mark you left in me
Helping me show others the impact

Of suicide grief
And letting others know
They are not alone
And we can continue this grief process

Together

Because you loved
Because you existed
Because you lived
Because you influenced

Today together you and I
You in heaven
Me here
Are speaking truth

On suicide grief

So I say thank you
All is not lost
You left me the will
To go through the pain

So that others can understand
So that others can work through their healing
Find their path
Through this complicated unbearable grief

All is not lost
My beautiful princess
You are physically gone
But you live on

Through these words
Through my will to help others
Through my vision to teach others
Suicide grief can be fought through
The love you left behind

You still Exist

I have been a mess
For a very long time
Crying and crying
No peace

For so long
I have tried to beat
The inner battle
Of understanding

Struggling
And struggling
Living in the past
Living in the future

Hoping one day
I would wake up
From this living nightmare
And you dying was all a dream

And then it hit me
One day I will die
The only separation
Is location

I am on earth
And you are in the sky
You exist in my love for you
In my heart that beats

You cannot die
There are vivid
Memories that thrive
And feelings you manifested in me

These things continue
You are connected to both
My heart and soul
The mark you left me will forever live

So I may not hug you
Kiss you
hold you or
Laugh with you

But you know what
I can remember
I can sit and call you
Talk with you

I can still love you
Tears may fall
But you exist
You live in me

I cannot forget
The gratitude
for having loved you
And for you loving me

I may miss you
but this is temporary
One day we'll be together

Again
You still exist
And so long as
I can have faith in
This truth

It is not over
It is not the end
It is not a spiritual death
It is not eternity
Because you live

Cup in the light

You had
A heart of beauty
That filled this world
with your existence and charm

Your compassion
And empathy brought hope
To those who needed love
You filled other people's cups

You believed in others
And breathed inspiration
In their lives
To this day although dead

You are bringing light to the world
To all the people you touched
To all the people you helped
To all the ones you healed

The way you loved us
The ones blessed enough
To be your family
Will always be remembered

We are forever grateful
For we had the privilege to watch you grow
Witness your little eccentricities
And your artistic ways
We saw how hard you worked

And yet it hurts
That you are gone
I need to remember the gifts
You left behind

And though everyday
I wish I could wrap
Myself around you
I was honored
to have known and loved you

I miss You

Beautiful light of my heart
Oh how I wished we had more time
To gaze at your precious smile
And look at your piercing eyes

If I could just hold you,
Fill your heart with joy
We could laugh one more time
Dance to your favorite song

Make your special cake
Get Ice cream and joke
My precious Angel
Your heart was too good
Too pure
For this world

I am sorry I could not see
Your hurt
Your pain
Your sadness
Your struggles

The only peace
The only consolation is
You are flying high
Happy
Joyous
Free

It is not the end
My love
When it is my time
I will see your face
Again

Smile, laugh,
Hear your sass
Your sarcasm
All in good fun

I will hold on to the hope
That we are here
Together
And that love
Transcends death

I love you
My sweet girl
Till I hold you
Wrap you
With my arms
Once again

My heart will be full
Knowing that I once
Held you near
And today I feel you
Here in my heart

Amends

I am sorry my dearest one
If ever I saddened your heart
Or I did not show you love

I am sorry that I was not there
In the moments of your silent pain
I wish I had known

I am sorry we lived far
And I did not make enough of an effort
To see you and laugh with you

I am sorry I did not call or text
I thought I had more time
I should have done more

I am sorry my beautiful
Sweet girl
This is my amends to you

For anything I have ever done wrong
For being a bad example
With broken relationships

For taking to drinking
For my answers
For being defined by a man

I am sorry my precious girl
For taking forever to learn
And rebuild my life

And my commitment to you
Is to make a living amends
By making you proud

I love you

Heart, body, and soul
And you make up the best of me
I am trying to help others
And it is because of you
Every single day of my life

I am determined to live
By touching other people's lives
Through your story
And that keeps you alive

Epilogue

This book was the hardest thing I have ever written. I cried so much in the process of writing, and my heart ached consistently. At times it was overwhelming, but I had my friends and family uplifting me every step of the way. I had my brother calling me five to six times a day to see how I was doing. I put myself on the line with my students, and many of them were cheering me on. This book was too important not to finish because so many people going through suicide grief or having friends and loved ones experiencing these losses do not understand how to support us. I tried to capture the moments of grief as I experienced them.

I wrote this book in a month because I was avoiding the task because the grief was too painful. Even with a deadline looming, I had to step away from the writing because the tears were flowing and flowing. As hard as they were, the tears were very healing. After a day of intense writing, I would reward myself by spending time with loved ones and working on being grateful for the blessings I do have. Although in the midst of grief, it is really difficult to see the light in the darkness. I never realized how much I loved my loved one, and going through the process of writing this book I realized what a loss we all experienced in losing her. Even after this book, I am still not in the acceptance stage. As I mentioned in a previous poem, I am an alcoholic and I am most grateful that this experience of a suicide loss did not send me into a relapse. In working a 12 step program, I am fully aware that acceptance is the answer to all of my problems, but I am not there. In working a 12-step program, I have come to accept that God and I do not agree on this issue. I do not agree with her death, and God did not save her like he saved me with my suicide attempt. For my sobriety, I have to have a relationship with God, and although I raged at him because of this; I have come to accept that it is okay to disagree with God, and he can handle it. I am not a religious person, I am more of a spiritual person, so I do believe my loved one is with the angels in heaven. That is a belief that I wholeheartedly believe and that gives me glimmers of peace.

I go to suicide survivors groups and I am surrounded by people just like me who have lost a loved one to suicide. I am not alone in my grief journey, and I do have hope that one day my brain will lead me to acceptance. I think that is why groups are so important because you can see what your progress can look like if you do the work through others who are farther ahead in their journey. The biggest blessing from the groups has been total acceptance and understanding of everything I am feeling. I think this type of loss is different than any other because there is guilt attached to it. I do feel guilty for what happened, but the feelings are not as intense as they were a year ago. It has been exactly a year and a half since she passed, and I feel guilty for not reaching out enough, for not knowing her mental health battle, for not holding her when she cried herself to sleep at night, and for not making the effort I feel I should have done while she was alive. I have hope that I will one day reach the point of acceptance in that too. I loved her deeply and the thought of reversing time constantly contaminates my brain, but there is really nothing that I could really do, and I am not in acceptance of that either, but healing takes work and if I give my grief what it needs I will get to a better place. Do not get me wrong, my life will never be the same. That woman that existed before she died will never exist again. I am a different woman, and I am not the same person, and although this death has taken pieces of me. I am working hard to learn to live with this loss. There are days I will struggle to shower or get out of bed, and that is okay. I try to give myself grace.

I am here in this world because there are people here that need me, and my purpose is to help others, so I am here because I still have work to do. Until I lost my loved one, I never knew the pain left behind from suicide, and what it has done for me is cured me from my suicide ideation. Those thoughts try to creep in from time to time, but I am more equipped to put them at bay because I do not want anyone to feel the way I have felt due to this loss. For this, I am extremely grateful.

For husbands, wives, friends, and family members of suicide survivors please be patient. Grief is complicated and difficult, and what we need from you is unconditional acceptance and love. You cannot fix it or heal us, and we know you have good intentions, but when you're at a loss of words, just say I love you and I am here. The grief is going to come at unexpected times and places please be understanding it is very difficult to control the pain. There have been times where I am having an amazing day, and then all of a sudden a song comes on that reminds me of her, and then I begin to cry. We do not do this on purpose. It is simply grief that comes at us, and our body reacts with tears. It is not your job to make us feel better, and the best thing you can say is that I am here and I love you. Please do not lecture us because although you think you may be right, we are doing the best we can with this immense pain that we carry. I know it is difficult to live with someone like us, but please understand that a lot of times we blame ourselves, and that is a big burden to bear. Do not say do not feel guilty like in a previous poem if we knew how to stop feeling guilty we would.

The truth is, it is a process. From what I have seen in others who are farther along in their journey than I am, they no longer feel guilty, but I do. For those who have to live with a grieving person due to suicide loss please be patient. This loss is heavy and it takes time and work to enjoy life again. Remember we did not choose this to happen to us, and so do your best to give us grace. Losses like this can pull out our toxic behaviors and at times it can separate us from family and friends. Understand suicide loss is different because we are left in shock, with so many unanswered questions, and at a loss not knowing how to make sense of it.

The tragedy of suicide can be absolutely overwhelming, and we are not the same person we were before this loss. Please do not force us to go to parties or holiday functions. Sometimes we cannot celebrate because of this loss. It is not personal, we are just doing the best we can. Sometimes we need to be alone. It is hard for people to see us grieving and crying and so we sometimes would rather deal with our grief alone. We are just trying to keep our head above water, so please be understanding as much as you can. Please do not tell us that their death was a sin. We believe from the bottom of our hearts that our loved one was in too much pain to continue with their life, and we wholeheartedly believe they are in heaven, with the angels, with God, or with nature. Please do not ask us if we missed any signs, think about that if we for one second saw the signs maybe this would not have happened, and we already feel too much guilt already. This happened and we did not cause it, we could not cure it, and we could not control it, so the only thing we can do is find our way through this awful complicated grief from suicide.

Resources

THE AMBER CRAIG MEMORIAL FOUNDATION
Dedicated to Suicide Prevention
P.O. Box 550 Placentia, CA 92871 • www.withhopefoundation.org

With Hope, the Amber Craig Memorial Foundation\
Friends With Hope Suicide Bereavement Support
Group
www.withhopefoundation.org
PO BOX 550
Placentia, CA 92871

Offerst suicide survivors support groups and
Bereavemetn services
https://www.tatianashope.org/services/

contact : beverly@tatianashope.org

Survivors of Suicide

TOGETHER WE SHARE

Offer suicide survivors support groups

https://survivorsofsuicide.us/

If you or someone you know is suffering from suicide ideation please call the crisis line and dial
988

Please tell someone who can help

Tell them:
You are loved, you are needed in this world,
Please get help, this world needs the beauty you bring. Sending prayers and love to all.

About the Author

Erica Castro is a Xicana English high school teacher who has taught for twenty seven years. She is dedicated to helping and empowering her students. She is a poet that feels that poetry can help people heal their inner-self. She has dedicated herself to publsihing student work. She published student art, poems, and story in the Oracle school anrhology. She has recently launched Daxson Publishing to publish marginalized voices. She has published Rosalilia M. Mendoza's *Lili of the Valley*, Adrian Fuerte-Campos *In Solace*. She is publishing her poetry book *The Pain Left Behind: Surviving a Suicide Loss*. She is also publishing *Creating Peace through the Grieving Process*, a book that helps you deal with the loss of a loved one. She is also publishing *Mariposa de Fuego: A Journey to Empowerment* by Peruvian born author Áurea María Altamirano Cuaresma coming out in July. Erica, has also participated in suicide attempt survival collaboration called *Alive to Thrive*. She has also written in two other book collaborations *Badass Within*, and *Healing and Growth: Inspiring Stories for Massive Transformation*. She just released another book collaboration called *Graceful Growth* Series about dealing with loss and grief of suicide.Her most recent book collaboration is called *Signs and Synchronicities*.

Connect with Erica: Instagram: ericalopez74

Publishers Note

Daxson publishing was created to help marginalized artists publish their work, so the world can hear their voice. The vision for this publishing house is to help people get their work out there, and not have them struggle finding their way through the publishing process. Everyone's voice deserves to be heard, and we are here to help. If you are interested in submitting a manuscript, email daxsonpublishing@gmail.com.

www.ingramcontent.com/pod-product-compliance
Lightning Source LLC
Chambersburg PA
CBHW051323120626
46547CB00015B/2370